The Story of a Special Day
Volume 19

January 19

January 19 is the nineteenth day of the year. There are 346 days remaining (347 in leap years) until the end of the year.

by Michael Dobson

Timespinner
Press

This book is also available in e-book form for Kindle, e-pub devices, and other formats from your favorite online booksellers.

For more information about the series, about us, or about your special day, please email us at editor@timespinnerpress.com.

Look for other volumes in *The Story of a Special Day,* coming often. See www.timespinnerpress.com for details and for the most recent information.

Table of Contents

For the definition of "O.S.," "N.S.," "CE," and "BCE" used with some dates , see the section "On Names and Dates."

Cover: A Gustave Doré illustration from Edgar Allan Poe's The Raven, along with a daguerrotype of Poe and a copy of his signature. Edgar Allan Poe was born January 19, 1809 — the PERSON OF THE DAY.

Quote of the Day

"Duty is the sublimest word in our language. Do your duty in all things. You cannot do more. You should never wish to do less."

Robert E. Lee, Confederate general
born January 19, 1807

Today
in
History
January 19

"Cruce de los Andes," by Julio Vila y Prades. General José de San Martin is on the left and General Bernardo O'Higgins on the right. The

What Happened on January 19?

From the creation of great works of engineering and art, to devastating wars and natural disasters, thousands of years of history have left their mark on each and every day of the year. Here are some important events that occurred on January 19. (Items with a photo or illustration are boxed.)

1817 — A combined group of Argentine and Chilean soldiers led by José de San Martin begin the **crossing of the Andes** in order to **liberate Chile** from Spanish rule. Over 4,000 soldiers set out, but a third were lost during the crossing. By using unexpected paths on their 21-day march, the army was able to enter royalist-held Chile without being noticed and were able to attack with complete surprise.

1853 — Giuseppe **Verdi's opera** *Il trovatore* premiers at the Teatro Apollo in Rome. It will become a major success and remains a classic of the operatic repertoire.

1883 — The **world's first electric lighting system using overhead wires, built by Thomas Edison,** begins operation in Roselle, New Jersey. The project demonstrated that an entire community could be lit by electricity.

1915 — In the **first major aerial bombardment** of a civilian target, German **zeppelins** bomb the English towns of Great Yarmouth and King's Lynn, killing at least 20.

A World War I poster created by the British government

1920 — The United States Senate votes **against the US joining the League of Nations**.

1937 — Howard Hughes sets a new transcontinental air speed record of 7 hours and 28 minutes, beating his own record time set a year previously.

Howard Hughes

1940 — In the **first Hollywood film to spoof Adolf Hitler**, *You Nazty Spy!*, starring the Three Stooges, premiers.

1953 — Nearly **72 percent of all television sets in the United States** tune in to *I Love Lucy* to watch the episode "Lucy Goes to the Hospital," in which she gives birth to Little Ricky.

1977 — US President Gerald Ford **pardons Japanese propaganda figure "Tokyo Rose."**

1946 mug shot of Iva Ikuko Toguri D'Aquino ("Tokyo Rose")

1978 — The **last Volkswagen Beetle made in Germany** is shipped. (Beetle production in Latin America continues until 2003.)

Advertisement for a 1968 Volkswagen Beetle

1983 — **Nazi war criminal Klaus Barbie** is arrested in Bolivia.

1983 — The **first Apple computer with a graphical user interface and a mouse, the Apple Lisa,** is released. Although it was a commercial failure, it introduced numerous features that would not appear on ordinary personal computers for many years.

1986 — The first IBM PC **computer virus** is released into the wild.

Quote of the Day

"They who dream by day are cognizant of many things which escape those who dream only by night."

Edgar Allan Poe, writer
born January 19, 1809

Births
and
Deaths
THER:
ACE.
MAGNA
January 19

Robert E. Lee. Lee was born January 19, 1807
(Photo: Julian Vannerson)

Notable January 19 People

With the current world population at about seven billion people, on average about 19 million people also celebrate their birthdays on January 19 — and that isn't counting millions and millions who came before! No matter when you were born, you share your birthday with many special people whose accomplishments (and occasionally embarrassments) have been noted as part of history.

In this section, you'll meet fascinating people who share your birthday. They're organized by what they're famous for, and then in reverse chronological order from most recent to earliest. Those who are shown in photographs or artwork have a box around them. We don't have photos of everyone, so please forgive us if your favorite person is missing.

Some of these people you've heard of, others will be new to you, but they all make up an important part of the reason that January 19 is a truly special day!

 Michael Dobson

From Edgar Allan Poe's *The Raven,* by Edouard Manet. Poe was born January 19, 1809

Cover Story/Person of the Day
Edgar Allan Poe (1809)

Edgar Allan Poe, born January 19, 1809; died October 7, 1849, is known for his poems and tales of mystery and the macabre, and is generally regarded as one of the great figures in American literature.

He is considered to be the inventor of detective fiction (the Mystery Writers of America's award is named the Edgar in his honor), made early contributions to science fiction, and was the first well-known American writer to try to earn a living through writing alone.

Poe's father abandoned his family when Poe was only one, and his mother died the following year. A Richmond, Virginia, family, the Allans, took him in as a foster child. He lived with the Allans until he entered university, and became estranged from his foster father over his gambling debts. Destitute, Poe joined the US Army as a private, and subsequently won an appointment to the US Military Academy at West Point. There, he was court-martialed for "gross neglect of duty and disobedience of orders," and was dismissed after a year.

His fellow cadets financed a volume of poems, raising $170, and Poe moved to Baltimore where he struggled financially while trying to write. His novel *The Narrative of Arthur Gordon Pym* was widely reviewed and was a moderate success. During his lifetime, he was best known as a critic.

In 1945, he published his most famous poem, "The Raven," which became a popular sensation — although he was only paid $9 for it. Other famous Poe works include "The Cask of Amontillado," "The Fall of the House of Usher," "The Masque of the Red Death," and "The Pit and the Pendulum," many of which were later filmed.

In October 1849, Poe was discovered on the streets of Baltimore, "delirious...in great distress, and...in need of immediate assistance." He was taken to the hospital, but never became coherent long enough to explain his condition, and died a few days later.

Illustration from "The Raven," by Gustave Doré

Self-portrait, Paul Cézanne

Who Was Born on January 19?

Art and Illustration

Thomas Kinkade, popular American painter and businessman known for successfully mass-marketing his work. *(1958)*

Joe Staton, comics artist and writer best known as illustrator of the daily *Dick Tracy* comic strip beginning in 2011; also created the superhero *E-Man* and illustrated numerous Marvel and DC comic titles, including the *Justice Society of America, Superboy and the Legion of Super Heroes,* and *Green Lantern. (1948)*

Paul Cézanne, French Post-Impressionist painter considered to be the bridge between late 19th century Impressionism and early 20th century art. Called "one of the greatest of those who changed the course of art history." *(1839)*

Business and Media

Paula Deen, celebrity chef and cooking show television host who operates The Lady & Sons restaurant in Savannah, Georgia; author of fifteen cookbooks. *(1947)*

Government and Politics

Martin Bashir, British journalist and political commentator for *MSNBC*, *Dateline NBC*, and *Nightline*. Resigned for "ill-judged comments" about vice-presidential candidate Sarah Palin. *(1963)*

Robert MacNeil, Canadian-American novelist and co-anchor of the PBS news program *The MacNeil/Lehrer Report*. *(1931)*

Javier Pérez de Cuéllar, 5th Secretary-General of the United Nations and subsequently Prime Minister of Peru. *(1920)*

Journalism and Letters

Patricia Highsmith, American novelist known for her psychological thrillers, including *Strangers on a Train* and *The Talented Mr. Ripley*, both of which were made into successful films. *(1921)*

Alexander Woolcott, American critic and commentator for *The New Yorker* magazine, a member of the Algonquin Round Table and the inspiration for the main character in the play *The Man Who Came to Dinner*. *(1808)*

Lysander Spooner, American political philosopher and abolitionist, early advocate of the labor movement. *(1808)*

Auguste Comte, philosopher who developed the doctrine of positivism; sometimes called "the first philosopher of science." Credited by some for coining the word *altruisme* (altruism). *(1798)*

Military

Robert E. Lee, American general who commanded the Confederate Army of Northern Virginia during the American Civil War, considered a postwar icon respected by both sides. *(1807) (Photo page 10.)*

Music

Dewey Bunnell, singer-songwriter and guitarist best known as a member of America; wrote such hits as "A Horse With No Name" and "Ventura Highway." *(1952)*

Robert Palmer, English singer-songwriter whose hits include "Addicted to Love," "Simply Irresistible," and "I Didn't Mean to Turn You On." *(1949)*

Dolly Parton, country singer-songwriter whose hits include "Jolene" and "Coat of Many Colors." Actress in such films as *9 to 5*, *The Best Little Whorehouse in Texas,* and *Steel Magnolias. (1946) (Photo next page)*

Janis Joplin, legendary rock singer-songwriter who died of a heroin overdose at the age of 27. Her hits include "Me and Bobby McGee," "Piece of My Heart," and "Mercedes Benz." *(1943) (Photo next page)*

Dolly Parton (left, with Carol Burnett)

Janis Joplin

The Everly Brothers, **Phil Everly** (left) and Don Everly (right)

Ish Kabibble

Phil Everly, known for his partnership with his brother Don as The Everly Brothers, whose hits include "Wake Up Little Susie" and "Bye Bye Love." Member of both the Rock and Roll Hall of Fame and the Country Music Hall of Fame *(1939) (Photo previous page)*

Lester Flatt, American bluegrass guitarist best known for his collaboration with banjo player Earl Scruggs, known variously as The Foggy Mountain Boys or Flatt and Scruggs. Known to mainstream audiences for "The Ballad of Jed Clampett," the theme song for the television series *The Beverly Hillbillies. (1914)*

Ish Kabibble, American cornet player and comedian, appeared in numerous films, including *Thousands Cheer,* along with Gene Kelly. Born Merwyn Bogue, he took his stage name from a nonsense phrase from one of his comedic songs. *(1908) (Photo previous page)*

Performing Arts

Roger Ashton-Griffiths, actor best known as Mace Tyrell in the television series *Game of Thrones. (1957)*

Paul Rodruiquez, noted Mexican-American stand-up comic and actor. *(1955)*

Katey Sagal, actress known for the television series *Married... with Children, Futurama,* and *8 Simple Rules.* *(1954)*

Dino, Desi, and Billy. **Desi Arnaz Jr.** on drums (center)

Desi Arnaz Jr., child actor and musician, son of Lucille Ball and Desi Arnaz, co-stars of *I Love Lucy.* Desi was born on the same day as his fictional counterpart, "Little Ricky;*" also a drummer for the band Dino, Desi, and Billy. *(1953)*

---

* See page 4 for the broadcast, watched by 72% of television households.

Shelley Fabares, actress and singer noted for the 1962 hit single "Johnny Angel," and for her performances on *The Donna Reed Show* and *Coach.* *(1944)*

Shelley Fabares (left) and Paul Petersen , *The Donna Reed Show*

Michael Crawford, stage actor and singer best known for originating the title role in *The Phantom of the Opera.* (1942)

Mike Reid, English comic actor best known for playing Frank in *EastEnders* and hosting the popular children's show *Runaround.* (1924)

Richard Lester, director known for his two films with the Beatles, *A Hard Day's Night* and *Help!*, as well as his work on the *Superman* film franchise. *(1932)*

Tippi Hedrin, actress and model primarily known for her work in two Alfred Hitchcock films, *The Birds* and *Marnie,* as well as 80 other films. *(1930)*

Nicholas Colasanto, actor primarily known for his role as "Coach" on the 1980s sitcom *Cheers. (1924)*

Jean Stapleton, character actress best known for playing Edith Bunker on the 1970s sitcom *All in the Family. (1923)*

Carroll O'Connor (left) and **Jean Stapleton** in *All in the Family*

James Watt, by Henry Howard

Science and Technology

Leonid Kantorovich (Леони́д Канторо́вич), Soviet mathematician who received the 1975 Nobel Memorial Prize in Economics for techniques used in the optimal allocation of resources; considered the founder of linear programming. *(1912)*

Sir Henry Bessemer, English inventor who developed the Bessemer process, the most important 19th century process for making steel, as well as numerous other inventions in iron, steel, and glass. *(1813)*

James Watt, Scottish engineer who developed the Watt steam engine, a major advance on previous steam engines, and the first design to be cost effective, making him a key contributor to the Industrial Revolution. He also developed the concept of "horsepower." The electrical "watt" is named for him. *[1736 O.S. (January 30 N.S.†)]*

Sports

Stefan Edberg, former world no. 1 tennis player from Sweden. *(1966)*

Minnesota Fats (Rudolf Wanderone), American Hall of Fame pool player and entertainer who took his name from the book and film The Hustler, claiming its main character was based on him (a claim denied by the book's author). Also known for his professional feud with rival pool player Willie Mosconi. *(1913)*

---

† James Watt was born January 19, 1736, according to the "Old Style" Julian calendar (in effect when he was born), but January 30, 1736 in the "New Style" Gregorian calendar. See "What Day of the Week is January 19?" for an explanation of different calendar types.

Associate Justice William O. Douglas (Photo: Harris & Ewing)

Who Died on January 19?

Art

Thomas Hart Benton, American regionalist painter, known for his scenes of everyday people primarily in the midwest US. *(1975)*

Government and Law

Harry E. Claiborne, US district court judge for Nevada; became the fifth person in US history to be removed from office through impeachment and the first federal judge sent to prison. *(2004)*

William O. Douglas, longest-serving associate justice of the US Supreme Court (over 36 years), called "the most doctrinaire and committed civil libertarian ever to sit on the court" by *Time* magazine. *(1980)*

Literature and Poetry

James Dickey, American poet and novelist best known for the 1970 book (and later film) Deliverance; 18th US Poet Laureate. *(1997)*

William Congreve, English comedic playwright and poet whose two most famous lines are mistakenly attributed to Shakespeare: "Music hath charms to sooth the savage breast" and "Hell hath no fury like a woman scorned." He also coined the phrase "kiss and tell." *(1729)*

Henry Howard, Earl of Surrey, English nobleman, known as one of the "fathers of the English sonnet." *(1547)*

Performing Arts and Music

Miguel Ferrer, actor known for roles in such films as *RoboCob* and *Iron Man 3* and for the TV series *Twin Peaks* and *NCIS: Los Angeles;* son of actor José Ferrer and singer Rosemary Clooney. *(2017)*

Ward Swingle, vocalist and jazz musician who founded The Swingle Sisters. *(2015)*

John Stewart, singer-songwriter; member of the Kingston Trio; wrote "Daydream Believer" for The Monkees. *(1980)*

Suzanne Pleshette, actress best remember as Emily Hartley on the 1970s sitcom *The Bob Newhart Show.* *(2008)*

Denny Doherty, singer-songwriter best known as a member of The Mamas & the Papas; later host and voice artist for the children's television show *Theodore Tugboat.* *(2007)*

Wilson Pickett, soul and rock singer-songwriter whose best-known hits include "In the Midnight Hour," "Land of 1,000 Dances," and "Mustang Sally." *(2006)*

Anthony (Tony) Franciosa, film and television actor best known for the 1960s drama *The Name of the Game* and the 1984 series *Finder of Lost Loves.* *(2006)*

The Mamas and the Papas on *The Ed Sullivan Show,* 1968. From left: Michelle Phillips, Cass Elliot, **Denny Doherty,** and John Phillips

Wilson Pickett (advertisement for his single "Mr. Magic Man")

Hedy Lamarr, actress best known for such films as *Ecstasy* and *Samson and Delilah*; also a mathematician and inventor who developed one of the core technologies that led to modern Wi-Fi and Bluetooth systems, for which she was elected to the National Inventors Hall of Fame. *(1995)*

Hedy Lamarr, from *The Heavenly Body* (1944)

Carl Perkins, rockabilly singer-songwriter whose best known song is "Blue Suede Shoes." Member of the Rock and Roll Hall of Fame, the Rockabilly Hall of Fame, and the Grammy Hall of Fame. *(1998)*

Don Simpson, motion picture producer of such hits as *Flashdance, Beverly Hills Cop,* and *Top Gun. (1995)*

Gene MacLellan, Canadian singer-songwriter whose best known songs include "Snowbird" and "Put Your Hand in the Hand." *(1995)*

Philosophy and Religion

Bhagwan Shree Rajneesh, controversial mystic, guru, and spiritual teacher whose ashram in Oregon led to a series of legal battles and physical attacks. *(1905)*

Debendranath Tagore (দেবেন্দ্রনাথ ঠাকুর), Hindu philosopher and religious reformer who helped found the Brahmo religion. Called "one of the greatest religious geniuses this country [India] ever produced." *(1905)*

Sports

Earl Weaver, managed the Baltimore Orioles for 17 season and achieved a .583 winning percentage; member of the Baseball Hall of Fame. *(2013)*

Stan Musial, outfielder and first baseman who played 22 seasons for the St. Louis Cardinals, considered one of the greatest hitters in baseball history, inducted into the Baseball Hall of Fame in his first year of eligibility. *(2013)*

Stan Musial (1948 Bowman baseball card)

Max Bentley, ice hockey forward who played in the NHL for twenty years; member of the Hockey Hall of Fame and named one of the NHL's 100 Greatest Players of All Time in 2017. *(1984)*

Ray Harroun, American race car driver known for winning the first Indianapolis 500 race, in which he used a controversial new invention: the rear-view mirror. *(1968)*

Ray Harroun in 1911

Quote of the Day

"All the things I really like to do
are either illegal, immoral, or
fattening."

Alexander Woolcott, critic,
born January 19, 1887

Holidays
Around
the World
January 19

The POE TOASTER's traditional gifts at Edgar Allan Poe's tomb, 2008 (Credit: Midnightdreary)

Holidays Around the World

If you're looking for a reason to take your special day off, you should know that every single day is a holiday somewhere in the world! Here's some of what you can celebrate on January 19!

General Events

Confederate Heroes Day (Texas)
The state of Texas celebrates Confederate Heroes Day each January 19.

Kokborok Day (Tripura state, India)
Observed in honor of the Kokborok language, an indigenous language in Tripura state and one of its official languages.

Poe Toaster (Baltimore, Maryland) *(photo)*
The "Poe Toaster" is either one or two unidentified people who has paid an annual visit to Edgar Allan Poe's grave in Baltimore each year for more than seven decades, where he would pour himself a glass of cognac and raise a toast to Poe, then leave three roses along with the rest of the bottle of cognac. Dressed in black with a wide-brimmed hat and scarf, his identity is unknown, though it is believed he passed the tradition along to his son.

Robert E. Lee Day (Alabama, Arkansas, Florida, Georgia, and Mississippi)

Confederate General Robert E. Lee is honored in several Southern states on January 19.

Food Holidays

In the United States, almost every day of the year is dedicated to a particular food. (Some other countries also have official food days, but only in America is there one every single day!) Sponsored by manufacturers, retailers, farmers, or simply fans, these days are often proclaimed by the President, Congress, state governors, or mayors. Given that there are more different foods than days of the year, some days honor more than one kind of food!

In the US, January 19 is **National Popcorn Day** (*photo*). Popcorn is both the most popular and the most profitable snack food. It dates back to at least 3600 BCE. Six different towns claim to be the "Popcorn Capital of the World," but there is no official victor.

In addition, the entire month of January is used to celebrate numerous foods.

- California Dried Plum Digestive Health Month
- Fat Free Living Month
- National Hot Tea Month
- National Oatmeal Month
- National Slow Cooking Month
- National Soup Month
- National Baking Month

- National Fat Free Living Month

And while we're on the subject of food, January is also **Weight Loss Awareness Month**, in case you've already forgotten those New Year's resolutions.

Popcorn (Credit: Cyclonebill)

Religious Feast Days and Holidays

Feast of Sultán (Bahá'í Faith)

Celebrated on the first day of the seventeenth month
of the Bahá'í calendar, held on January 19 most years.
This feast celebrates the power of sovereignty and
the most potent of rulers.

Saint Days

Each day in the year is a feast day for various saints.
They are somewhat different in western Christianity
(Catholicism and many forms of Protestantism) and
in eastern (Orthodox) Christianity.

In *Western Christianity*, January 19 is the feast day
of Saints Bassianus of Lodi, Henry of Uppsala,
Marius, Martha, Audifax, Abachum, Pontianus of
Spoleto, and Wilfstan of Worcester.

In *Eastern Orthodox Christianity*, it is also the
commemoration of the Mark of Ephesus, as well as
feasts for Saints Euphrasia of Nicomedia, Theodotus,
Arsenius of Kerkyra, Firminus, Contestus, Laumer,
Branwalader, Nathalan, Remigius of Roen,
Arcontius, Catellus, and Macarius the Roman of
Novgorod. (These people are honored on January 6
by "Old Calendrists."‡)

---

‡ "Old Calendrists" use the Julian, rather than the Gregorian,
calendar for liturgical purposes. For an explanation of different
calendar types, see "What Day of the Week is January 19?"

Theophany (Orthodox Christianity) *(photo)*

The Orthodox Christian feast day of Theophany commemorates the baptism of Jesus on both sides of the Jordan River, and is equivalent to the feast of Epiphany (marking the visit of the Magi to the Christ child) in Western Christian traditions. The date of the feast in the modern Gregorian calendar is January 6, but "Old Calendrists" observe the feast on January 19.§

"The Concecration of Water on the Theophany," Boris Kustodiev

§ For an explanation of different calendar types, see "What Day of the Week is January 19?"

Timkat (ጥምቀት) (Ethiopian Orthodox Church)

Timkat is the Ethiopian Orthodox celebration of Epiphany, held on the 10th day of the Ethiopian month of Kerr (January 19 most years; January 20 in leap years).

Vodici (Водици) (Republic of Macedonia)

Orthodox Christian communities in the Republic of Macedonia celebrate Jesus's baptism on January 19.

Honorary Months

Presidents, Congresses, and nations around the world issue proclamations recognizing particular months to honor certain causes. These events generally fall in January, though honorary months do come and go. Holidays established by states and nonprofit organizations are listed if verified. If not otherwise specified, all months are US. There is some variation from year to year; some celebratory months get added and others get dropped. Two places to get up to date information are the current edition of *Chase's Calendar of Events* or the website Brownielocks. Here are some honorary designations for January.

- Adopt a Rescued Bird Month
- Bath Safety Month
- Be Kind to Food Servers Month
- Birth Defects Month
- California Dried Plum Digestive Month
- Cervical Health Awareness Month

- Financial Wellness Month
- Get Organized Month
- International Child-Centered Divorce Awareness Month
- International Creativity Month

- National Braille Literacy Month

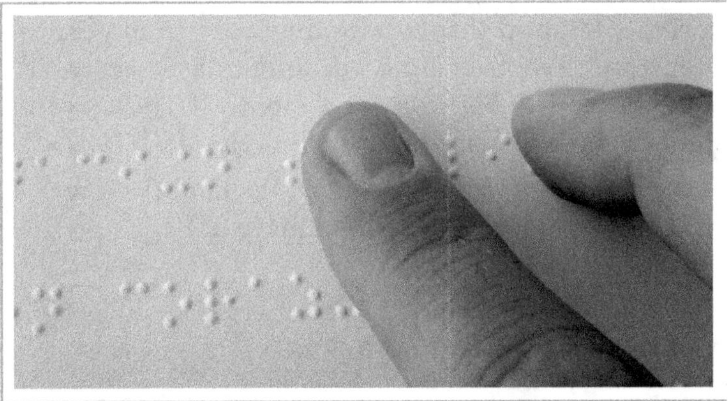

A person reading a braille book, for National Braille Literacy Month (Photo: Antonio X Alonso CC BY-SA 2.0)

- National Clean Up Your Computer Month
- National Codependency Awareness Month
- National Mentoring Month
- National Polka Music Month
- National Poverty in America Awareness Month
- National Skating Month
- National Thank You Month
- National Volunteer Blood Donor Month
- Slavery and Human Trafficking Prevention Month

- Stalking Awareness Month
- Teen Driving Awareness Month
- Train Your Dog Month (also Walk Your Dog Month)

Moveable and Multi-Day Events

Some events take place over a specific week or time period. Start and finish dates may vary from year to year. Some events occur on different days each year (such as "fourth Saturday of a month"). These events sometimes take place on or include January 19.

- *Bóndadagur* (Husband's Day), Iceland (Friday between January 19 and January 25)
- Diet Resolution Week
- Silent Record Week
- New Year's Resolution Week

Week Long Celebrations that Sometimes Include January 19

- Hunt for Happiness Week (third full week)
- National Fresh Squeezed Juice Week (third full week)

Just For Fun

Anyone can make up a holiday, and many people do! These holidays are unofficial, and some of them come and go, but here are a few more reasons to celebrate on January 19!

- Thank Your Mentor Day
- Tin Can Day

January, by Eugène Grasset

Quote of the Day

"It's easy to kill a movie. Just move it to January."

Mike Myers, as "Dr. Evil"
from the *Austin Powers* movies

About
the
Month
of
THE[R]
AC
MAGNA
January

"January," from the *Brevarium Grimani* by Simon Bening (c.1510)

January: The First Month

That blasts of January
Would blow you through and through.

— *William Shakespeare*, The Winter's Tale

January wasn't always the first month in the year. In ancient Rome, March was the first month until about 450 BCE. Even after January became the official first month in the calendar, Romans still counted dates from the inauguration of the consuls, March 15 and May 1.

In the Middle Ages, Christian feast days were used to start the new year, including March 25 and December 25. It wasn't until the 16th century that European nations made January 1 the official start of the new year. (This was called "Circumcision Style" because January 1 was also celebrated as the Feast of the Circumcision of Jesus.)

The name January (*Ianuarius*) is derived from the Roman god Janus, the god of beginning and transitions. Janus gives his name to the Latin word for door (*ianua*), because January is the door to the year. Janus is normally portrayed as having two faces, one looking toward the future and one toward the past. In spite of that, the goddess Juno was the patron of that month.

In both the Julian and Gregorian calendars[**], January is the first month of the year and one of seven months with 31 days. In the Northern Hemisphere, January is the coldest month of the year, and in the Southern Hemisphere, it's the warmest, equivalent to the Northern Hemisphere's July.

January in Other Cultures

The month of January has different names in different languages. Some nations use calendars other than the Gregorian, and their months may overlap with January. In lunar-based calendars, such as the Islamic calendar, months move through the seasons. Still, many languages often have a word for January itself.

Albanian: Janar

Anglo-Saxon: Wulf-monath

Arabic (Egypt, Sudan, Yemen): يونأغيناير (*yanāyir*)

Arabic (Levant): حزيركانون الثاني (*kānūn al-thānī*)

Arabic (Libya): الصهنار (*aynu n-nār*)

Arabic (Algeria and Tunisia): جأينجانفي (*Jānfī*)

Arabic (Morocco): غيناير (*yanāyər*)

Azerbaijani: Yanvar

Basque: Urtarril

Bulgarian: януари (*januari*)

[**] To learn more about the different calendar types, see "What Day of the Week is January 7?"

Chinese: 一月 (Cantonese: *yātyuht*; Mandarin: *yīyuè*; Taiwanese: *it-goeh*)

Corsican: Ghjennaghju

Croatian: Siječanj

Czech: Leden

Finnish: Tammikuu (oak moon)

French: Janvier

German/Danish/Norwegian/Slovenian: Januar

Greek: Ιανουάριος (*Ianouários*)

Haitian Creole: Janvye

Hebrew: ינואר (*yanû'ar*)

Hindi: जनवरी (*janvarī*)

Hungarian: Január

Irish (Gaelic): Eanáir mí Eanáir

Italian: Gennaio

Japanese: 一月 (*ichigatsu*), 睦月 (*mutsuki*)

Kazakh: Қаңтар (*Ķaņtar*)

Korean: 일월 (*ilweol*)

Lithuanian: Sausis

Maori: Kohitātea

Old English: Se æfterra Gēola

Polish: Styczeń

Portuguese: Janeiro

Russian: январь (*janvar'*)

Scottish Gaelic: am Faoilleach

Sesotho: Pherekgong

Slovene: Prosinec

Spanish: Enero

Swahili/Dutch/Swedish: Januari
Swazi: Bhimbidvwane
Thai: มกราคม (*makarakhom*)
Turkish: Ocak
Vietnamese: 腩义 (*tháng một*)
Walloon: Djanvî
Welsh: Ionawr
Yiddish: אויגויאַנואַר (*yanuar*)
Zulu: uJanuwari

Mengapa? Zašto? 为什么呢？
Por quê? Чаму? Чому?
Poukisa? کیوں؟ Per què?
Tại sao? Miks?
Bakit? Kial? למה?
Waarom? Hvers vegna?
どうして？ פאַרוואָס? Niyə?
Warum? Dlaczego? Pourquoi?
Ինչու? Зашто? چرا؟ Quid?
Cén fáth? Pam?
Zergatik? რატომ? Miért?
Kwa nini? Proč?
Hoekom? क्यों?
De ce? Kodėl?
เพราะเหตุใด Защо? Why?
Perché? Miksi?
لماذا؟ Prečo? Varför?
Għaliex? Γιατί;
¿Por qué? Pse?
왜? Почему? Зошто?
Kāpēc? Neden?
Hvorfor? 為什麼呢？

January Sayings and Superstitions

Here are some sayings and superstitions associated with the month of January.

New Year Superstitions

- It's important to kiss those dearest to us at the stroke of the New Year to keep their affections for the next twelve months.

- The new year must not be seen with bare cupboards. Stock up on supplies and make sure there's plenty of money in ever wallet in the home.

- Do not begin the new year with the household in debt.

- The first person to enter your home after the stroke of midnight will tell you the kind of year you will have.

- Do not let anything leave your house on the first day of the year, not even garbage.

- Start your year off with good luck by eating hoppin' john, a dish made with black-eyed peas and rice (southern United States).

- Wear something new on January 1.

- Be sure to open the door at midnight to let the old year escape.

- Babies born on New Year's Day will always have good luck.

January Wedding Superstitions

- A January bride will be a prudent housekeeper, and very good tempered.

- Married in January's hoar and rime/Widowed you'll be before your prime.

- Married when the year is new, he'll be loving, kind and true.

January Symbols

Birthstone: Garnet, representing constancy.

Soviet postage stamp showing a geologist finding garnets

Birth Flower (Britain): Carnation, representing love, fascination, and distinction

Vase with Red and White Carnation on a Yellow Background,
by Vincent van Gogh

Birth Flower (America): Carnation or Snowdrop (*Galanthus*)

A New Year's greeting card with snowdrops

Birth Flower (China): Plum blossom (*prunus mume*)

Red Plum Blossom (Photo: Frank Gualtieri)

Birth Flower (Japan): Camellia

Camellias (Clara Maria Pope)

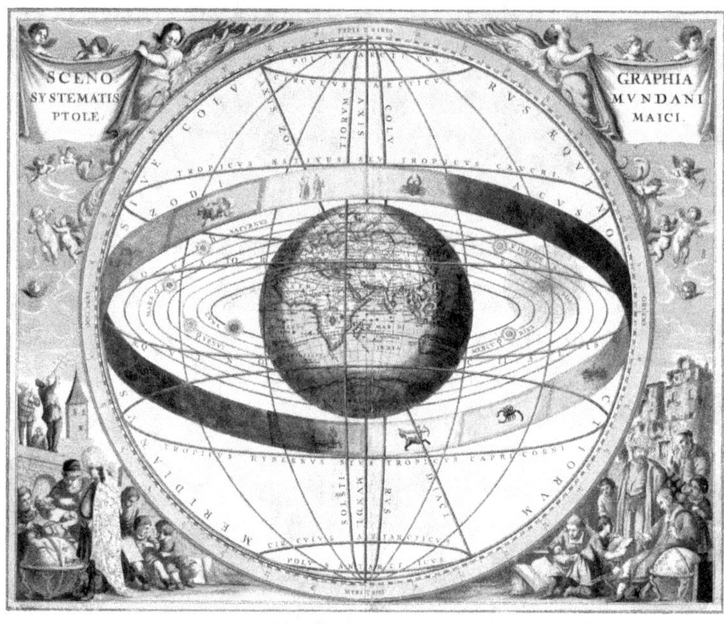

Scenography of the Ptolemaic Cosmography, by Johannes van Loon, based on Andreas Cellarius's *Harmonia Macrocosmica*, 1660

January 19 Zodiac Signs

From the perspective of someone on Earth, the Sun appears to move through the sky throughout the year, along a path astronomers call the *ecliptic plane*. The ecliptic plane is divided into twelve constellations, known as the zodiac, based on traditionally observed patterns of stars. On your birthday, you can't see your constellation, because it's in the daytime sky.

The zodiac was first developed by Babylonian astronomers about 2,500 years ago. Because they were unaware that the Earth wobbles like a spinning top (known as *precession*), they didn't make allowance for the fact that the Sun's path through the zodiac changes over time.

That means there are now two sets of dates for your birth sign. The *tropical dates* are the original Babylonian dates; the *sidereal dates* tell you where the Sun actually appears as it moves along its annual path.

January 19 is unusual in that both the tropical and sidereal signs are the same — **Capricorn!**

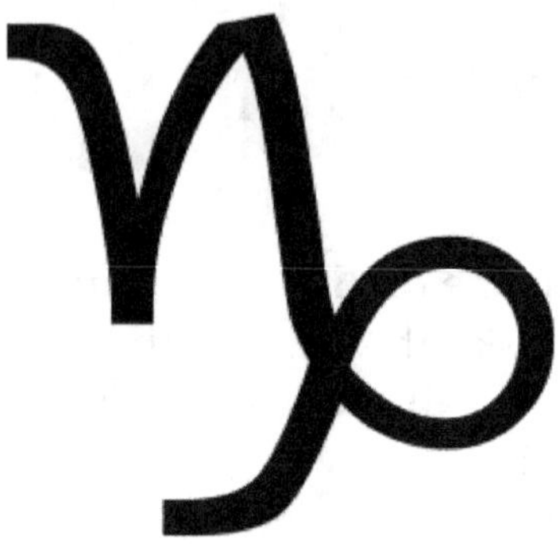

Capricorn

Tropical December 22 to January 20
Sidereal January 15 to February 14

The origins of the constellation Capricorn date back
to Sumeria and Babylonia. Based on Enki, the
Sumerian god of wisdom and waters, Capricorn has
the head and upper body of a mountain goat and the
lower body and tail of a fish. The mountain goat
represents ambition and intelligence, the fish
represents passion and spirituality.

An earth sign, Capricorn is ruled by the planet
Saturn. They are often thought to be responsible,
patient, ambitious and loyal, but can sometimes be
seen as conceited, distrusting, and unimaginative.
Capricornians are supposed to be compatible with
Taurus, Pisces, and Virgo, but not with Aries,
Sagittarius, or Leo.

The Sign of Capricorn, by Giovanni Maria Falconetto (Courtesy Palazzo d'Arco, Mantua, Italy)

Illustration by Edward Penfield

What Day of the Week is January 19?

On what day of the week does January 19 fall?

Surprisingly, this isn't an easy question. Because the calendar year is 365 days long (366 in leap years), it doesn't divide evenly by the seven days of the week.

Also, the Earth goes around the Sun in about 365-1/4 days, so a calendar tends to drift over time. That's why the same date falls on different weekdays in different years.

This is made even more complicated by a change in calendars that took place in 1582. Our modern calendar has its roots in ancient Rome, in a calendar reform conducted by Julius Caesar. Caesar commissioned mathematicians to attack the problem, and they came up with the idea of leap years, and thus standardized the calendar for centuries to come. This was called the Julian calendar.

Over time, however, the small errors in Caesar's calculation compounded. That's why Pope Gregory XIII commissioned the Gregorian calendar, used in most of the world today. Some countries converted in 1582, when the calendar was first developed; some converted later; other still haven't changed.

Gregorian and Julian aren't the only types of calendars. The Hebrew year, the Islamic year, and many other calendars are used in different parts of the world and among different people.

You can convert Gregorian dates to other calendars, including the Hebrew calendar, the Islamic calendar, and even the Mayan calendar by visiting the Fourmilab Calendar Converter at http://www.fourmilab.ch/documents/calendar/.

Chinese calendar systems are quite complex and have changed several times; a full discussion is far beyond the scope of this book. If you're interested, you can find information here: http://www.hermetic.ch/cal_stud/chinese_cal.htm.

On Names and Dates

Historians use "CE" (Common Era) and "BCE" (Before the Common Era) instead of the more common "AD" (Anno Domini, or Year of Our Lord) and "BC" (Before Christ), reflecting the fact that the year-numbering system established by the Gregorian calendar is used throughout the world in many countries not culturally Christian.

The CE/BCE designation dates back to at least 1708, and has been adopted as a standard by the United Nations and the Universal Postal Union. Because this series of books covers events and people of all nations and cultures, we use the CE/BCE terms.

The abbreviation "O.S." ("Old Style") on some dates refers to the fact that the Russian Empire did not switch from the Julian to the Gregorian calendar at the same time as the rest of Europe, and therefore some figures and events have two dates.

Also, in the Julian calendar in England in the 16th century, the year began on March 25 rather than January 1. To avoid confusion with Gregorian dates, dates between January and March were often written using both years.

People and events whose original names are not in the Western alphabet have their native names (where possible) in the appropriate script shown in parenthesis. If you are using an e-reader to access an electronic version of this book, all characters don't always display on all devices.

A 50-year brass perpetual calendar.

Quote of the Day

"Time is an illusion, lunchtime doubly so."

Douglas Adams,
from *The Hitchhiker's Guide to the Galaxy*

Notes
and
Credits
Timespinner
Press

Cartoon by John T. McCutcheon

Copyright, Credit, and Contact

Follow Us

Our blog "This Day in History" (http://
timespinnerpress.com/this-day-in-history/) features short
articles on events and people associated with each day, and
updates several times each week. Also subscribe to the
"Quote of the Day" at http://timespinnerpress.com/quote-
of-the-day/. You can get daily links by following us on
Facebook at TimespinnerPress, or on Twitter as
@sidewisethinker.

Contact Us

Find an error or a format problem? Want information about
the series, about us, or about when the volume for your
special day might be available? Please email us at
editor@timespinnerpress.com. (We also take requests if your
special day isn't yet complete. Please give us at least six
weeks' notice if possible.)

Sources

We owe a great debt to Wikipedia, which is our first stop for
research. We attempt to make independent confirmation of
all important dates and facts through a variety of other
sources.

Other sources we frequently use include the Library of
Congress; "on this day" listings from *Encyclopedia Britannica*,
the *New York Times*, and the BBC; Omniglot for the names of
months in other languages; *Chase's Calendar of Events*; and, of
course, the always essential Google.

All art and photographs are either in the public domain, used under a Creative Commons license, or with a "fair use" justification, and most frequently come from Wikimedia Commons and the Library of Congress Prints and Photographs Division.

Attribution is provided where possible, or as requested by the copyright owner, or when there is particular historical significance, listed below. For information about any particular illustration or photograph, please contact us.

Credits

1. The front cover background illustration is from the Harper & Brothers 1884 edition of Edgar Allan Poe's *The Raven* is by Gustave Doré, courtesy of the Metropolitan Museum of Art. It is in the public domain under the Creative Commons CC0 1.0 Universal Public Domain Dedication.

2. The 1849 daguerrotype of Edgar Allan Poe used on the cover is in the public domain because its copyright has expired. The photographer is unknown.

3. The reproduction of the signature of Edgar Allan Poe used on the cover is from the 1885 book *Edgar Allan Poe* by George E. Woodberry. It is in the public domain because its copyright has expired.

4. The illustration of the month of January used on the back cover is from the French Gothic illuminated manuscript *Les Très Riches Heures du duc de Berry* by the Limbourg Brothers, Jean Colombe, and an intermediate painter whose name is lost to history.

5. The box graphic used on the first page is from a 1916 pamphlet entitled "Divorce versus Democracy" authored by G. K. Chesterton, originally published in London by the Society of St. Peter and St. Paul. It is in the public domain in the US because it was published prior to 1923, and is in the public domain in all countries (including the country of origin) in which the copyright time is the author's life plus 70 years or less.

6. The graphic design for the section pages in this book is from a design originally created for a pharmacy label. It is from Wellcome Images (ICV No 11073, photo V0010813), and is used here under CC BY-SA 4.0.

7. The 19th century painting "Cruce de los Andes" by Julio Vila y Prades is in the public domain because its copyright has expired.

8. The British World War I zeppelin poster is from the Library of Congress Prints and Photographs Division, digital ID cph. 3g10972. It is in the public domain in the UK because it was created by the UK government prior to June 1, 1952, and in the US because it was first published before January 1, 1923.

9. The photograph of Howard Hughes is in the public domain because it was published in the US between 1923 and 1977 and without a copyright notice.

10. The mug shot of "Tokyo Rose" is in the public domain as a work created by an officer or employee of the US government as part of that person's official duties.

11. The image of a 1968 Volkswagen 1500 was released into the public domain by its creator.

12. The 1864 portrait of Robert E. Lee was taken by Julian Vannerson, and is in the public domain because its copyright has expired. It is from the Library of Congress Prints and Photographs Division, digital ID cwpb.04402.

13. The 1875 illustration from "The Raven" by Edouard Manet is in the public domain because its copyright has expired.

14. The illustration of *The Raven* is by Gustave Doré. It is in the public domain because its copyright has expired.

15. The 1890 self-portrait of Paul Cézanne is in the public domain because its copyright has expired.

16. The 1980 photograph with Dolly Parton and Carol Burnett is in the public domain because it was published in the US between 1978 and 1989 without a copyright notice, and its copyright was not subsequently registered. Frequently, publicity photographs are not copyrighted because of the way they are intended to be used.

17. The 1969 publicity photograph of Janis Joplin is in the public domain because it was first published in the US between 1923 and 1977 without a copyright notice. Traditionally,

publicity photographs are not copyrighted because of the way in which they are intended to be used.

18. The 1958 publicity photograph of the Everly Brothers is in the public domain because it was first published in the US between 1923 and 1977 without a copyright notice. Traditionally, publicity photographs are not copyrighted because of the way in which they are intended to be used.

19. The publicity photograph of Ish Kabibble is in the public domain because it was first published in the US between 1923 and 1977 without a copyright notice. Traditionally, publicity photographs are not copyrighted because of the way in which they are intended to be used.

20. The 1965 publicity photograph of Dino, Desi, and Billy is in the public domain because it was first published in the US between 1923 and 1977 without a copyright notice. Traditionally, publicity photographs are not copyrighted because of the way in which they are intended to be used.

21. The 1962 publicity photograph from *The Donna Reed Show* is in the public domain because it was first published in the US between 1923 and 1977 without a copyright notice. Traditionally, publicity photographs are not copyrighted because of the way in which they are intended to be used.

22. The 1976 publicity photograph from *All in the Family* is in the public domain because it was first published in the US between 1923 and 1977 without a copyright notice. Traditionally, publicity photographs are not copyrighted because of the way in which they are intended to be used.

23. The 1797 portrait of James Watt by Henry Howard is in the collection of the Naitonal Portrait Gallery, London. The image is in the public domain because its copyright has expired.

24. The Harris & Ewing portrait of William O. Douglas was taken after 1930, and is from the Library of Congress Prints and Photographs Division, digital ID cph.3a44775. According to the Library, there are no known copyright restriction on this work.

25. The 1968 photograph of The Mamas and the Papas performing on the *Ed Sullivan Show* is in the public domain

because it was first published in the US between 1923 and 1977 without a copyright notice.

26. The trade advertisement for Wilson Pickett's single "Mr. Magic Man" originally appeared in the February 10, 1973, issue of *Billboard*. It is in the public domain because it was first published in the US between 1923 and 1977 without a copyright notice.

27. The 1944 publicity photograph of Hedy Lamarr in *The Heavenly Body* is in the public domain because it was first published in the US between 1923 and 1977 without a copyright notice. Traditionally, publicity photographs are not copyrighted because of the way in which they are intended to be used.

28. The 1948 Bowman baseball card of Stan Musial is in the public domain because it was first published in the US between 1923 and 1963, and although there may or may not have been a copyright notice, the copyright was not renewed.

29. The 1911 photograph of Ray Harroun is in the public domain because its copyright has expired.

30. The 2008 photograph of Poe's grave along with the traditional gifts of the Poe Toaster, is by "Midnightdreary." It is used here under CC BY-SA 3.0.

31. The 2008 photograph of popcorn is by "Cyclonebill," and is used here under CC BY-SA 2.0.

32. The 1921 painting by Boris Kustodiev is in the public domain because its copyright has expired.

33. The photograph of a person reading a braille book was taken by Antonio X. Alonso in 2009. It is used here under CC BY-SA 2.0.

34. The 1896 postcard "January" by Eugène Grasset is in the public domain because its copyright has expired.

35. The 1815 woodcut of a Regency era wedding proposal is in the public domain because its copyright has expired.

36. The painting *January* is from the *Brevarium Gremani*, circa 1510, and is in the public domain because its copyright has expired.

37. The graphic of "Why" in several languages was created in 2011 by "Maierstrahl," and is used here under CC BY-SA 3.0.

38. The 1968 USSR postage stamp "Prospecting Geologist with Found Diamond and Red Crystals-Pyropes (Garnets)" is not an object of copyright according to Part IV of Civil Code No. 230-FZ of the Russian Federation (2006).

39. The 1886 painting "Vase with Red and White Carnations on a Yellow Background" by Vincent Van Gogh is in the public domain because its copyright has expired.

40. The German New Year's greeting card was made circa 1900. It is in the public domain because its copyright has expired.

41. The 2006 photograph of a red plum blossom (*prunus mume*) was taken by Frank Gualtieri, who released the photograph into the public domain.

42. The illustration of camellias by Clara Maria Pope is from Samuel Curtis' *Monograph on the Genus Camellia*, published in 1819. It is in the public domain because its copyright has expired.

43. The celestial sphere is from *Scenography of the Ptolemaic Cosmography*, by Johannes van Loon, based on Andreas Cellarius's *Harmonia Macrocosmica*, 1660. It is in the public domain because its copyright has expired.

44. *The Sign of Capricorn*, by Giovanni Maria Falconetto, created 1468, can be found in the Palazzo d'Arco, Mantua, Italy. It is in the public domain because its copyright has expired.

45. The 1906 automobile calendar is by Edward Penfield, and is in the collection of the Library of Congress Prints and Photographs Division. It is in the public domain because its copyright has expired.

46. The 50-year perpetual calendar photograph is in the public domain.

47. The cartoon by John T. McCutcheon is from his 1905 collection *The Mysterious Stranger and Other Cartoons by John T. McCutcheon*. It is in the public domain because its copyright has expired.

48. "January," by Hans Thoma, is from his book *Festkalender*. It is in the public domain because its copyright has expired.

License Description and Terms

Aside from material purely in the public domain, photographs and other material in this book are used under specific licenses permitting free use, usually with an attribution requirement. For full text and terms of these licenses, click or enter the appropriate links below. If you believe there is an error in the copyright status or attribution of any of these images, please email us.

- Creative Commons Attribution 2.0 Generic (CC-BY 2.0): http://creativecommons.org/licenses/by/2.0/deed.en
- Creative Commons Attribution-Share Alike 3.0 Generic (CC-BY-SA 3.0): http://creativecommons.org/licenses/by-sa/3.0/
- Creative Commons Attribution-Share Alike 2.5 Generic (CC-BY-SA 2.5): http://creativecommons.org/licenses/by-sa/2.5/deed.en
- Creative Commons Attribution-Share Alike 2.0 Generic (CC-BY-SA 2.0): http://creativecommons.org/licenses/by/2.0/deed.en
- Creative Commons Attribution-Share Alike 1.0 Generic (CC-BY-SA 1.0): http://creativecommons.org/licenses/by-sa/1.0/deed.en
- CC0 1.0 Universal (CC0 1.0) Public Domain Dedication (CC0 1.0) http://creativecommons.org/publicdomain/zero/1.0/deed.en
- GNU Free Documentation License (GFDL): http://en.wikipedia.org/wiki/Wikipedia:Text_of_the_GNU_Free_Documentation_License
- License Art Libre (Free Art License): http://artlibre.org

 Michael Dobson

"January," by Hans Thoma

Other Books from Timespinner Press

The Story of a Special Day

Michael Dobson

A series of (eventually) 366 volumes covering everything that happened on your special day! Events, births, deaths, quotes, holidays, and much more. It's like a birthday card they'll never throw away!

US$7.95 print / US$2.99 ebook.

From Plassey to Pakistan

Humayun Mirza

The history of British Colonial India and the formation of Pakistan from the unique perspective of the son of Pakistan's first president and last of the royal line of Bengal, Bihar, and Orissa! This unique historical document tells the inside story of this distinguished family, including the detailed story of the coup that toppled his father from power!

US$27.95 print

A Whole New Navy: America's War in the Pacific

Miles Durr

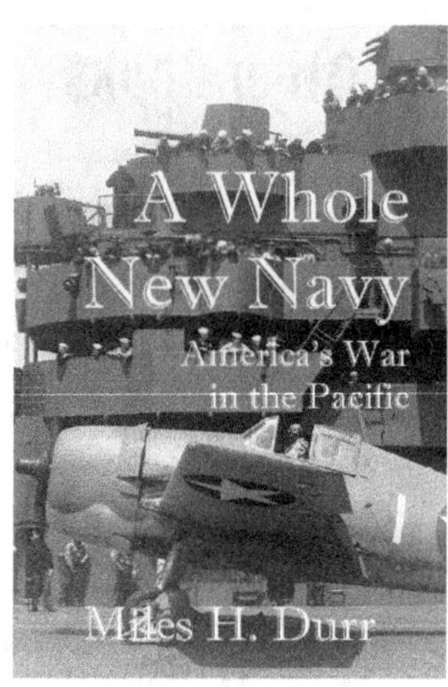

The most comprehensive and detailed description of America's naval war in the Pacific ever—every battle, every ship, every task force and every task group from Pearl Harbor through the Japanese surrender! A must-have for the collection of every World War II buff!

US$29.95 print

Improbable History: The Weird, the Obscure, and the Strangely Important

edited by Michael Dobson

From the birth of Western civilization to the rescue of Apollo 13, from the Leaning Tower of Pisa to Florence's Duomo, history has often turned on small, improbable details. Whatever happened to the ancient Samaritan people? Why did a fortuitous rainstorm allow the British to conquer India? How did an air raid in Italy lead to the development of chemotherapy? What happened when Albert Einstein met Adolf Hitler on the streets of Berlin? How did the Japanese manage to attack the US mainland using balloons? A cast of award-winning writers tackle some of the strangest tales in history!

US$19.95 print

The Letters of William Philip Schwartz 1842-1855

edited by John F. Schwartz

The 19th century soldier and adventurer William Philip Schwartz wrote a series of vivid and detailed letters chronicling his adventures in the Indian Wars, the Mexican-American War, the Gold Rush, and his term as Marine sergeant aboard the USS Constellation. A pioneer in photography, he took *the first known war photographs*. An unforgettable first-hand look into life in the 19th century!

US$17.95 print

Timespinner
Press

www.timespinnerpress.com